The Flavors of Phillies Nation

The Flavors of Phillies Nation

A Philadelphia Tailgate Companion

Edited by

Brian Michael

iUniverse LLC.
Bloomington

THE FLAVORS OF PHILLIES NATION
A PHILADELPHIA TAILGATE COMPANION

iUniverse books may be ordered through booksellers or by contacting:

iUniverse
1663 Liberty Drive
Bloomington, IN 47403
www.iuniverse.com
1-800-Authors (1-800-288-4677)

Because of the dynamic nature of the Internet, any web addresses or links contained in this book may have changed since publication and may no longer be valid. The views expressed in this work are solely those of the author and do not necessarily reflect the views of the publisher, and the publisher hereby disclaims any responsibility for them.

Images property of the respective copyright holders and Phillies Nation, Brian Michael

Recipes found in this book are credited to the individual(s) that submitted the recipe. We maintain no copyright over these recipes and authors agreed to have their recipes published in the book.

We are not responsible for the outcome of any recipe you try from this. While we have reviewed each recipe carefully, you may not always achieve the results desired due to variations in ingredients, cooking temperatures, typos, errors, omissions, or individual cooking abilities. We are not responsible for any domestic accidents, fires or food poisoning that could result from preparation of the recipes, eating of raw eggs, meat and fish. We are not responsible for any kind of food borne disease. The recipes are intended for use by persons having appropriate technical skill, at their own discretion and risk. We assume no obligation or liability, and makes no warranties, with respect to these recipes.

Any trademarked names are used only to identify the ingredients in the recipe.

Phillies Nation, LLC is not affiliated with Major League Baseball or the Philadelphia Phillies.

ISBN: 978-1-4759-8248-0 (sc)
ISBN: 978-1-4759-8250-3 (hc)
ISBN: 978-1-4759-8249-7 (e)

Printed in the United States of America

iUniverse rev. date: 03/25/2014

This book is dedicated to my mom (the best cook), my dad
(the biggest Phillies fan), and anyone who can relate.

Contents

Foreword

Tailgating unites two of Philadelphia's greatest passions: food and sports. The zeal that Philadelphians bring to the pursuits they care about is unparalleled. I should know: I witnessed it firsthand during my fourteen years in center field.

The fervor and the excitement fans bring to the ballpark for a big game are also evident at the Stephen Starr–Garry Maddox Barbecue Challenge, an event I host at Citizens Bank Park each year to raise funds for inner-city youth. It's well known that I take my barbecue seriously, but the participants in our event raise smoking and grilling to an art form. Since our contestants are tailgaters as well, I know the competitive spirit I see at the Barbecue Challenge thrives at parties taking place on game days throughout the season. We're not just out to win on the field, we're out to conquer at the grill.

Hopes run high and loyalties run deep in this town, but even greater are the heart and the compassion of those who live in the Greater Philadelphia region. I'd like to thank the members of our community who shared a recipe for this collection, which benefits Philabundance and its effort to reduce food insecurity among the nine hundred thousand local residents at risk for hunger and malnutrition.

Whether you're a newcomer to the world of tailgating or a

seasoned pro, I invite you to enjoy the recipes herein and taste the passion that inspired them.

—Garry Maddox

Editor's Introduction

This book is filled with recipes from some of the biggest Phillies fans around. In February 2010, we asked the readers of PhilliesNation.com to send in their favorite tailgating recipes with the simple idea of putting them together in a fan-inspired book. As the recipes poured in, we started to see distinctions: some were for pregame cooking in the parking lots, some were for at-home game-watching parties, some were vegetarian, and some were new twists on old classics. But they were all Philly. More specifically—Phillies.

There is no denying that some of the most serious tailgating takes place at college and professional football games around the country, with huge smoker trailers, elaborate furnished spaces, and enough beer to fill the Schuylkill. Yet this book focuses on a more nuanced approach to tailgating, a more baseball style of tailgating. The recipes presented here are from Phillies fans and have a Phillies attitude. And if you don't know what that means, head down to South Philly on a warm summer evening, fire up your grill, and serve up one of these delicious tailgate treats.

Oh, and don't forget to bring an ice-cold cooler full of your favorite frosty beverage. This book pays particular attention to tailgate-friendly beers. Our friends at Barleydine.com and the Grey Lodge in Northeast Philly offer their recommendations for classic tailgate brew. Plus, we have a whole section dedicated to cooking with our sudsy friends.

Finally, to help put to rest all those alcohol-induced and profanity-laced arguments over tailgating facts, we've got some of them too. Pat Gallen shares the history of tailgating in America, while Nick "the Beerman" shows you the best places around the park to set up shop. And for a walk down memory lane, I researched an article about the history of tailgating in the old Phillies ballpark, Connie Mack Stadium.

So please enjoy reading, cooking, and having fun with this book. If you have ideas or questions about it, visit www.philliesnation.com/cookbook.

Go Phils!

—Brian Michael

The History of Tailgating

If you research the history of the tailgate, you'll find it began just a short trip up Route 1 in New Brunswick, New Jersey, during a Rutgers–Princeton football game. The year was 1869, and it forever changed the way sporting events would be enjoyed. What began as a college football thing slowly transitioned into a baseball experience as well. In the 1920s and '30s, the pregame ritual came into its own, with fans dressing in their Sunday finest and women sporting their hometown team's colors by way of corsage.

As the automobile became more popular through World War II, so did the tailgate experience. Making it easier for fans to celebrate before the sporting event, cars gave people a way to mix the two. According to Stephen Linn, author of The Ultimate Tailgater's Handbook, this practice is where the term "tailgating" was born. Perhaps because of the baby boom of the 1950s, the station wagon was the ultimate vehicle for the family. It also allowed the pregame party to go mobile.

The tailgate as we know it rounded into form in the 1980s, as gas grills became smaller and easier to transport and parking lots turned into welcoming havens for the fanatical fan who would show up complete with flags, team gear, and, in recent times, a television. The evolution of the gas-powered generator has allowed for a whole assortment of electronics to come along for the ride.

Fast-forward to our present-day gatherings, which now involve monster grills, elaborate motorized coolers, and an array of entertaining recreational opportunities (cornhole, anyone?). Prior to a sporting event, it's almost a given that you'll find a pigskin flying through the air, no matter the sport taking place inside the stadium.

But the tailgate is not exclusive to contests that use a ball or bat. "Deadheads" made tailgating a must for concertgoers in the '60s and '70s, when drugs, sex, and rock and roll were part of the pregame menu. Nowadays, good luck finding a show in the summer months that does not include some sort of entertainment beforehand in the lots.

Whatever the occasion, tailgating can be an exciting way to begin your game-day (or concert-day) experience. There's nothing like the camaraderie of sharing an ice-cold beverage, a burger, and a dog alongside some of your best friends and fellow worshippers. To some, it's become just as, if not more, important than the game itself.

See you in the parking lot!

—Pat Gallen

Tim Malcolm and Pat Gallen at our
2011 Opening Day tailgate.

Beer Pairing

Tailgating, on some level, accompanies just about every major sporting event. Whether you're in the lot or at your house, the following suggestions are aimed at improving your tailgating experience. This book is jam-packed with terrific recipes that tantalize the tailgater in all of us. If you want to take these foods one step further, pairing the right beer can launch your palate into a world of culinary nirvana. We've picked what we find to be some of the most common beer styles that would accompany any tailgate. We've briefly described each style and given you pairing suggestions to get you started. This is by no means a rulebook; we encourage you to experiment with your pairings.

Pairing Types

There are two methods to pairing beers:

1. Complementary: Match characteristics of the beer with characteristics of the food—maltiness with meat, bitterness with spice, or maltiness with sweetness. Examples: Brown ale with grilled steak, IPA with Thai or Mexican, stout with chocolate cake.
2. Contrasting: Let the characteristics of the beer differ from those of the food—maltiness with spicy heat, bitterness with extreme dessert sweetness, acidity with

sweetness. Examples: Brown ale with Mexican, IPA with carrot cake, framboise lambic with cheesecake.

Beer and Food Interactions

Some things to remember when selecting beers to go with your food:

- Hop bitterness, roasted malt, alcohol, and carbonation balance sweetness, savory, and fat.
- Sweetness and maltiness balance spicy heat and acidity.
- Hop bitterness emphasizes spicy heat.

Beer and Food by Style

American Pale Ale: Gorgeous amber-colored beers with awesome, creamy heads. A fair amount of hop bitterness that balances well with the sweet malt flavors.

- Examples: Oskar Blues Dale's, Troegs, Upslope
- Pairing Suggestions: Calamari, cheeseburger, chili, mac and cheese, nachos, pizza, shrimp

American IPA: Much of the same characteristics of the pale ale, although these things will punch you in the tongue. Loaded with hop bitterness that usually overpowers any malt sweetness. Moderate to high alcohol content.

- Examples: Victory HopDevil, Stone Ruination, Sly Fox 113
- Pairing Suggestions: Chili, enchiladas, fajitas, nachos, salmon, salsa

American Lager: Very light body and highly carbonated. Low malt flavor and very low hop flavor; usually made with corn and/or rice. Very low alcohol.

- Examples: Miller, Budweiser, Coors

- Pairing Suggestions: Bratwurst, salad, calamari, chicken, clams, eggs, seafood pasta, sushi

Classic Irish Dry Stout: Very dark beers that aren't too heavy on the tongue. High malt flavor with very low hop bitterness and low alcohol.

- Examples: Guinness, Young's, Murphy's
- Pairing Suggestions: Crab, ham, lobster, raw oysters, chocolate, fruit tarts

German Pilsner: Light golden, crystal-clear color with a nice punch of bitterness from the hops. Very light-bodied and usually quite low in alcohol.

- Examples: Pilsner Urquell, Victory Prima, Sly Fox Pikeland
- Pairing Suggestions: Baked ham, bratwurst, chicken, chowder, crab, salsa, shrimp

Hefeweizen: Light bodied, golden colored, and slightly cloudy. Characterized by the orange aroma, bready flavor, and huge white fluffy head. Very low alcohol.

- Examples: Magic Hat Circus Boy, Hoegaarden, Widmer Hefeweizen
- Pairing Suggestions: Eggs and bacon, sushi, salads, shrimp

Vienna Lager: Nice amber-colored beer with a moderate tan head. High flavor from malts with very low flavor from hops. Low in alcohol; great drinkability.

- Examples: Yuengling, Sam Adams
- Pairing Suggestions: Baked ham, mac and cheese, meat loaf, nachos, pizza, sausage, turkey

—Joshua Lepley

Top Ten Tailgating Beers

1. Oskar Blues Dale's Pale Ale—Fantastic flavor in a can
2. Victory Prima Pils—One hoppy pilsner
3. Sly Fox Route 113—Local flavor
4. Stone Arrogant Bastard—Not for the faint of heart
5. Dogfish Head 90 Minute IPA—Slammin' imperial IPA
6. Southern Tier Iniquity—Awesome pairing beer
7. Guinness Draught—Classic stout
8. Magic Hat Circus Boy—Light and refreshing
9. Yuengling Lager—Historical flavor
10. Miller Lite—You can drink a ton of it

—Joshua Lepley

Ten Tailgating Tips

1. Bring the essentials: grill (with fuel of choice), spatula, tongs, ketchup, mustard (spicy brown or yellow), cooler with ice.
2. Use cooking methods you usually employ at home. For instance, the versatility of a cast-iron skillet allows you to sauté, fry, and bake on your grill.
3. Use tailgate-friendly tools like presoaked wooden skewers instead of metal ones. Rather than bringing home dirty dishes and cups, take advantage of disposable options.
4. Do prep work at home and take advantage of travel time to marinate food.
5. Use premade marinades to save time and add flavor. This could be as simple as bringing a packet of Italian dressing to coat grilled wings or steak. You could also create your own jar of unique spices, and then just sprinkle the mixture on whatever you're grilling. Instant gourmet!
6. Having a huge tailgate with fifty or more people? Consider getting it catered by your favorite sandwich or BBQ shop.
7. Show up early. Most lots open at least two hours prior to game time, so get there early if you want the best spots

(for instance, under a tree, on grass, or near a bathroom, a trash can, or the ballpark).

8. Don't undercook your food. Understand the cooking times for the meat you are grilling or use a meat thermometer to test doneness.

9. On hot days, find or bring shade if possible and drink plenty of water. Offering only beer as an option on a steamy day in August just means you'll pass out in your seat by the fourth inning.

10. Have fun! Bring games like lawn darts, wiffle ball, cornhole (that beanbag toss game), or even just a baseball and some gloves. Likewise, share with neighbors. Ignore the stereotypes—Phillies fans are friendly fans. Look no further than the next parking space to learn new recipes and share the tailgate experience.

—Brian Michael

Recommended Internal Temperatures for Grilled Meat

There's nothing worse than getting sick and missing a crucial part of a game. When cooking, you always want to be sure not to cross-contaminate food and to cook your meat to a safe temperature. Follow these recommended temperatures for a safe tailgate.

Steak and Lamb

- Rare: 130°F
- Medium-rare: 130 to 140°F
- Medium: 140 to 155°F
- Medium-well: 155 to 165°F
- Well: 170 to 185°F

Ground Beef

- 160°F

Veal

- Medium: 145 to 155°F

Pork (like grilled pork chops)

- Medium: 140 to 155°F
- Medium-well: 155 to 165°F

- Well: 175 to 185ºF

Grilled Chicken and Turkey
- Dark meat (thigh, leg): 170 to 175ºF
- White meat (breast, wing): 160 to 165ºF

Fish
- Medium-rare: 120ºF
- Medium: 135ºF

—Brian Michael

Tailgating at Citizens Bank Park

When tailgating in Philadelphia, one word seems to stick out in almost everybody's conversations: Jetro. The Jetro lot is Party Central on football Sundays for Eagles games, and all spring and summer long as fans gather to pregame for the Phillies. The massive lot is a prime location, a corner's jump from Citizens Bank Park and right across the street from Lincoln Financial Field. With two front lots and a back lot that seems endless, this is the place to be in Philadelphia before a game. In recent years, the Phillies have cracked down on tailgating in the lots they own. But fear not, Philadelphia faithful, Jetro is there for you.

The best part about the Jetro lot is that nobody bothers you. Don't light anybody on fire, and odds are that nobody will come bother you about drinking your Yuenglings out of the bottle. No cups necessary … because, let's be honest, it just tastes better out of the bottle. Some of the more popular beers that you can find in the Jetro lot are the already mentioned Yuengling Lager and Flying Fish—and, believe it or not, Philadelphia is one of the few areas where Miller Lite is the domestic beer of choice. I should know, considering I'm "the Beerman." Once you get inside the ballpark, just witness me flying (or walking gingerly, depending on if I'm trying to pay attention to the game) up the steps of Citizens Bank Park with a cold case of Miller Lite on my head.

But what do you pair up with those ice-cold brews? Well, the pages of this cookbook will give you a few ideas that hopefully you'll find handy. My tailgate food of choice? I keep it simple— some hot dogs, smoked sausage, burgers, and my very own Chesapeake Bay Wings. That doesn't mean everybody keeps it simple in the Philly lots, though. Some of the things I've seen cooked and then devoured in the lots would make Gordon Ramsay's palate tingle: lobster tails broiled in butter, filet mignon with spinach, grilled teriyaki duck, and lastly, the one food that has left me more satisfied than anything anybody has ever cooked for me before a game: ham wrapped in sausage wrapped in bacon. Infreakingcredible.

Food and drink ... only one thing is missing: drinking games. Whether it's beer pong, flip cup, or even washers, you are bound to find some sort of game being played throughout the lots. Don't forget to factor in the wind on those games of beer pong, or you are in for a long afternoon. In one of my favorite tailgating moments last season, we had a sixty-person game of flip cup that took place over four folding tables. Madness.

Next time you are in the lots and you see a bright yellow "Beerman" jersey with 124 on the back, shout me a holler. I'd love to throw a quick one down and steal some of your grub on my way into the ballpark.

—Nick "the Beerman" Staskin

Tailgating and Phillies Ballparks

The tailgates we know today around the parking lots of South Philly are a far cry from how fans pregamed when the ballparks were located in much more residential North Philly. Whereas fans of the current generation set up a grill and cooler in the parking spot next to their car, our parents and grandparents preferred a frosty mug and sandwich in the corner saloon or on the comfort of their own stoop. Of course, there were the dismal days between 1920 and 1933 when Prohibition ruled and the Phillies carried a .384 winning percentage. The current generation should consider itself lucky.

For the first half-century of the Phillies' existence, the team bounced around various hometown fields—including Recreation Park, the grounds of the University of Pennsylvania, and Columbia Park—before settling in the Baker Bowl in 1887. Twenty-two years later and just five blocks away, Shibe Park opened as the home of the Athletics of the American League. Eventually the Phillies moved to Shibe during the 1938 season, solidifying North Philadelphia as the epicenter of baseball in the city.

Before games at Shibe Park, Phillies fans could patronize the shops and restaurants that lined Lehigh Avenue and Twenty-First Street on the first level of the stadium. Matt Kilroy, a personal friend of Connie Mack and a famous professional player in the nineteenth century, opened a bar at the corner of Twentieth and Lehigh. Kilroy's quickly became a hangout for fans and players both before and after games. Although Kilroy sold the bar in 1935, the spot remained a Phillies pregame institution.

The importance of tailgating to past generations cannot be overstated, since it was not until 1961 that beer finally became legal at Connie Mack Stadium (even though the American league legalized it in 1901). Furthermore, beer was not available for Phillies Sunday games until 1972.

Since the stadium was situated in a residential neighborhood, there were no parking lots in which to fire up a grill or throw back a few beers. This lack of parking is eventually what forced the Phillies to move to South Philadelphia with its spacious and plentiful lots—which set the stage for the tailgate we know and love today.

—Brian Michael

For more information on the history of Phillies tailgating, check out:

- Bruce Kuklick, To Every Thing a Season: Shibe Park and Urban Philadelphia, 1909–1976
- Rich Westcott, Philadelphia's Old Ballparks

The Basics

We start with a mix of recipes that are appropriate for tailgating either at the ballpark or in the comfort of your own home. The recipes in this chapter represent a great way to get started with tailgating concepts and flavors.

A hat tip goes out to Kelli Amato for providing many of these recipes and allowing the Phillies Nation crew to test the results.

Four-Layer Tex-Mex Dip

Ingredients

- 2 8-ounce blocks cream cheese
- 2 15-ounce cans refried beans
- 2 15-ounce cans chili (beef, turkey, or veggie)
- 1 16-ounce package taco or Mexican shredded cheese (2 cups)
- Tortilla chips, for serving

Directions

1. Preheat your grill to 350°F.
2. In a 9-by-12-inch pan, spread the cream cheese in an even layer.
3. Spread the refried beans for another even layer. (You may not need the full two cans.)
4. Spread the chili on top of the beans.
5. Put the pan on the grill and cook for 12 minutes. Then layer on the shredded cheese until melted.
6. Serve with tortilla chips.

Very simple, but I'm considered "famous" for this dip. Most people don't know the under layer!

—Kerry Budd
Conshohocken, PA

Italian Hoagie Dip

Ingredients

- 1/2 pound cooked ham, thinly sliced
- 1/2 pound Genoa salami, thinly sliced
- 1/2 pound mortadella, sliced
- 1/2 pound capicola, sliced
- 1 pound processed American cheese, sliced
- 2 cups mayonnaise
- 2 teaspoons dried oregano
- 1 onion, chopped
- 1/2 head iceberg lettuce, shredded
- 2 tomatoes, diced
- 12 hoagie rolls, torn into pieces

Directions

1. Tear the ham, salami, mortadella, capicola, and cheese into pieces and place in a large bowl.
2. In a medium bowl, stir the mayonnaise and oregano.
3. Add the mayonnaise mixture to the meat mixture 1/2 cup at a time, mixing in until the meat and cheese are well coated.
4. Mix in the onion.
5. Refrigerate for at least two hours.
6. Before serving, mix in the iceberg lettuce and tomatoes.
7. Serve with the hoagie roll pieces for dipping.

Serves about 20 people.

—Jeff Costello
Mount Laurel, NJ

Philly Beans

Ingredients

- 1 28-ounce can vegetarian baked beans
- 1 sweet onion, grated
- 1/4 cup Karo dark syrup
- 1/4 cup dark brown sugar
- 1/4 cup ketchup
- 3 tablespoons spicy mustard
- Love of the Phillies

Directions

1. Add baked beans to an old-fashioned cast-iron skillet.
2. Add in all of the other ingredients and mix gently.
3. Bake, uncovered, at 350°F for 45 minutes or until bright red, sticky, and delicious!

—Barbara Boland
Oley, PA

Buffalo Chicken Dip

Ingredients

- 1 cup celery, finely chopped
- 2 teaspoons vegetable oil for sautéing
- A pinch of salt and pepper
- 2 12.5-ounce cans chicken
- 2 packages cream cheese
- 6 ounces wing sauce, such as Crystal or Texas Pete
- 1 cup cheddar cheese, shredded
- 8 ounces blue-cheese dressing

Directions

1. In a saucepan over medium heat, sauté the celery in the oil with a pinch of salt and pepper until soft.
2. Drain water from the cans of chicken and break up the chicken in a bowl. Add to the celery.
3. Add in the cream cheese, stirring constantly.
4. Add in the wing sauce, cheddar cheese, and blue-cheese dressing.
5. After the mixture is thoroughly heated, put the dip in a baking dish and bake in the oven at 350°F for 15 minutes covered, and then 15 minutes uncovered.

This dish can be served in a chafing dish for parties or in a foil pan heated on the grill for tailgating. Serve with tortilla chips (scoops work best).

—Michael Powers
Collegeville, PA

Pepperoni Dip

Ingredients

- 1/2 6-ounce bag sliced pepperoni
- 1 10.5-ounce can cream of mushroom soup
- 1 8-ounce block cream cheese, softened
- Tortilla or bagel chips, for serving

Directions

1. Preheat oven to 350°F.
2. Cut pepperoni slices into fourths and mix with the soup and cream cheese.
3. Bake for 15 to 20 minutes.
4. Serve with tortilla or bagel chips.

—Kelli Amato
Phoenixville, PA

Golden Artichoke Dip

Ingredients

- 1 envelope onion-soup mix
- 1 14-ounce can artichoke hearts, drained and chopped
- 1 cup real mayonnaise
- 1 8-ounce container sour cream
- 1 cup shredded Swiss or mozzarella cheese

Directions

1. Preheat oven to 350°F.
2. In a 1-quart casserole, combine all ingredients and mix.
3. Bake 30 minutes or until heated through.
4. Serve with your favorite dippers, like French bread or tortilla chips.

—Kelli Amato
Phoenixville, PA

Awesome Wings

Ingredients

- 12 to 15 frozen chicken wings
- 1 stick butter
- 3 packages dry Italian-dressing mix
- 1/2 cup hot sauce

Directions

1. Bake the wings at 400°F for about 1 1/2 hours until golden brown.
2. In a separate pan, melt the butter, the dressing mix, and the hot sauce, mixing together.
3. Pour the mixture over the wings and broil for 5 minutes.

Delish!

—Maria Orr
Broomall, PA

White Pizza Dip

Ingredients

- 1 package Lipton Recipe Secrets Savory Herb with Garlic soup mix
- 1 16-ounce container sour cream
- 1 8-ounce tub ricotta cheese
- 1 cup shredded mozzarella cheese (about 4 ounces)
- 1/4 cup (1 ounce) chopped pepperoni (optional)
- 1 loaf Italian or French bread, sliced

Directions

1. Preheat oven to 350°F.
2. Pour the soup mix in a shallow 1-quart casserole.
3. Mix in the sour cream, ricotta, 3/4 cup of the shredded mozzarella, and the pepperoni.
4. Sprinkle with the remaining 1/4 cup mozzarella.
5. Bake uncovered for 30 minutes or until heated through. Serve with the bread.

—Kelli Amato
Phoenixville, PA

Chesapeake Bay Wing Sauce

Ingredients

- 1 stick butter
- 2 12-ounce bottles Steve's & Ed's Buffalo Wing Sauce
- 3 tablespoons Old Bay Seasoning
- 1 teaspoon oregano

Directions

1. Melt the butter in a pan over medium heat.
2. Pour both bottles of wing sauce into the melted butter.
3. Fill one bottle of wing sauce halfway with water and add to the sauce and butter, mixing together.
4. Add the Old Bay and oregano.
5. Heat for 5 minutes and mix with approximately 60 cooked wings, or use for dipping.

—Nick "the Beerman" Staskin
Sicklerville, NJ

The Beerman flipping burgers outside RFK
Stadium at our 2008 DC road trip.

Dessert Pretzel Dip

Ingredients

- 8 ounces cream cheese, softened
- 1 stick butter
- 1 cup sugar
- 1/2 16-ounce bag pretzel sticks
- 8 ounces caramel sauce
- 4 Granny Smith apples

Directions

1. Spread the cream cheese across a plate. (It's easier when the cream cheese is softened ahead of time.)
2. Melt butter in a pot on medium heat. Add sugar to make a creamy soup-like caramel sauce. (You don't want to add too much sugar, or it won't coat the pretzels.)
3. Break up the pretzel sticks into little bits.
4. Add the pretzel bits to the melted butter mixture.
5. Mix quickly.
6. Spread the pretzel mixture on top of cream cheese.
7. Pour the caramel sauce over the top of the pretzel mixture. Use as much or little as you want. Pretzels do not need to be completely covered.
8. Serve with the apples for dipping.

—Kelli Amato
Phoenixville, PA

Homemade Guacamole

Ingredients

- 2 ripe avocados
- 1 ripe tomato, seeds and pulp removed, chopped
- 1/2 red onion, chopped
- 1/2 cup cilantro leaves, finely chopped
- 1 or 2 jalapeños, stems and seeds removed, diced
- Juice of 2 limes
- 1/2 teaspoon coarse salt

Directions

1. Cut avocados in half. Remove the pits. Scoop out avocado from the peel into a mixing bowl.
2. Using a fork or potato masher, mash the avocado.
3. Combine the tomato, onion, cilantro, jalapeños, lime juice, and salt, and fold them into the mashed avocado.
4. Add more salt, lime juice, or cilantro, to taste.
5. Cover with plastic wrap directly on the surface of the guacamole to prevent oxidation from the air reaching it. Refrigerate until ready.

—Liz Gossens
Washington, DC

**Liz enjoying a Shorty's cheesesteak at our
2010 New York Mets road trip**

Cole Slaw

Ingredients

- 1 head Napa cabbage, julienned
- 1/4 cup red cabbage, shredded
- 2 carrots, grated
- 1/4 cup apple-cider vinegar
- 1 tablespoon honey
- 1 teaspoon salt
- 1/2 cup mayonnaise
- 1 tablespoon Dijon mustard
- 1 teaspoon celery seeds

Directions

1. Mix all the ingredients together in large bowl (or plastic container if you're bringing it to the game).
2. Let stand 5 minutes before serving.

—Kelli Amato
Phoenixville, PA

Homemade Salsa

Ingredients

- 5 Jersey tomatoes
- 1 large white onion
- 1/2 cup loosely packed cilantro leaves
- 2 medium bottles hot sauce
- 2 lemons
- 1 1/2 tablespoons olive oil
- 1/2 tablespoon each salt and black pepper
- 1 1/2 tablespoons white vinegar

Directions

1. In a food processor, chop the tomatoes, onions, and cilantro separately.
2. Place all chopped ingredients in large mixing bowl.
3. Add hot sauce.
4. Squeeze out the juice of 2 lemons and add it to the salsa.
5. Add the olive oil, salt, pepper, and vinegar.
6. Mix the salsa well.
7. Chill for 1 hour before serving.

—Kelli Amato
Phoenixville, PA

At the Ballpark

These recipes are perfect for a tailgate party outside the ballpark before a Phillies game.

Don't forget to pack all of your essential gear, including your favorite grill and a fully stocked cooler.

Helen's Salsa Cornbread

Ingredients

- 2 boxes Jiffy corn muffin mix
- 2 extra-large eggs, as needed for preparing cornbread mix (the bigger the egg, the better the batter)
- 2/3 cup milk, as needed for preparing cornbread mix (can be stored in a premeasured container according to cornbread recipe on box)
- 1/2 cup cut corn (fresh is best, but defrosted frozen corn works also)
- 1 24-ounce bottle corn oil
- 1 16-ounce jar salsa

Tools

- 9-inch or larger cast-iron skillet

Directions

1. Preheat your grill to 350°F. (You will be baking on a grill.)
2. Combine the cornbread mix, milk, and eggs as indicated in the instructions on the box.
3. Pour oil into the skillet, making sure you have about 3/4 inch of oil filling the skillet.
4. Pour in the cornbread batter until it is about 3/4 inch from the top of the skillet. (The mixture will rise as it cooks.)
5. Now pour the salsa on top of the mixture in any design you like. (It doesn't really matter; the salsa will settle and spread into the middle of the cornbread as it cooks.)

6. Place the skillet on the grill and close the cover. (If your grill does not have a cover, you can use a large deep tinfoil chafing pan.)
7. Let the cornbread cook without looking for 35 minutes. (If you peek, you'll have to wait longer for it to fully cook.).
8. When the edges of the cornbread are browned, it's done.
9. Remove from the heat and let sit uncovered; let cool before serving.

This won second place chef's choice in the 2006 Garry Maddox challenge.

—Kevin, Barbara, and Helen Kilmartin
Philadelphia, PA

Ginger Sesame BBQ Chicken

Ingredients

- 6 boneless, skinless chicken-breast halves
- 1 tablespoon sea salt

Marinade

- 1/4 cup rice wine vinegar
- 2 tablespoons soy sauce
- 1/4 cup olive oil

Sauce

- 1 cup Newman's Own Low-Fat Sesame Ginger Dressing
- 2 cloves garlic, minced
- 1 shallot, chopped

Directions

1. Make the marinade: Combine the wine vinegar, soy sauce, and oil. Add the chicken and marinate overnight in the refrigerator.
2. Make the sauce: Mix the dressing, garlic, and shallot in a bowl.
3. Grill the chicken on medium heat for 16 minutes (a total of 8 minutes per side).
4. During the last 5 minutes on the grill, smother the chicken with the sauce and sea salt.

—Joseph Roache
Philadelphia, PA

Tailgate Dogs

Ingredients

- 1 sweet onion, chopped
- 3 ounces cola
- 1 teaspoon cracked black pepper
- 6 hot dogs
- 6 hot-dog buns
- 6 ounces Philly cream cheese
- Sriracha (Thai hot sauce)

Directions

1. Caramelize the sweet onion in a pan on low to medium heat using the cola and cracked black pepper. The cola really adds a nice sweetness to the onions, which comes into play later. Doing the onions at home ahead of time makes this an even friendlier tailgate recipe.
2. Grill your hot dogs.
3. When ready, toast a hot-dog bun and spread on some Philly cream cheese. (Using the spreadable or whipped sometimes can make this easier.)
4. Place a hot dog on the bun, top with some of the caramelized onions, and then add Sriracha to the top.
5. Repeat with the remaining hot dogs and buns.

—Curt Decker
Nodding Head Brewery & Restaurant
1516 Sansom Street
Philadelphia, PA

Zucchini Dogs

Ingredients

- 1 zucchini
- 1 hot-dog bun
- Condiments

Directions

1. Cut a zucchini in half the long way.
2. Grill it (skin-side up, flesh side against the grill).
3. Serve it in a hot-dog bun with your usual hot-dog fixings—or even better, with some hummus.

—Tracey Rich
King of Prussia, PA

Tulsky's Coma-Inducing BBQ Chicken

Ingredients

- 1 tablespoon paprika
- 1 tablespoon garlic powder
- 1/2 teaspoon cayenne pepper
- 1/2 teaspoon ground mustard seed
- 1/2 teaspoon cinnamon
- 1 teaspoon kosher salt
- 1 teaspoon freshly ground black pepper
- 4 pounds chicken legs and wings, bone-in
- 2 to 3 bottles of your favorite BBQ sauce

Directions

Prep Cooking at Home

1. Preheat oven to 350°F.
2. Mix together all of the dry ingredients and make a rub.
3. Coat the raw chicken with the rub and give it a generous rubdown.
4. Place the chicken in a large baking pan and bake in the oven for 25 to 30 minutes.
5. Take the chicken out of the oven and let it cool for about 10 minutes.

Finishing at the Ballpark

6. Fire up your charcoal grill and preheat for 20 to 30 minutes.
7. Pour the BBQ sauce into a large mixing bowl and dip the baked chicken in the bowl.
8. Place directly on the grill, close lid, and let cook for about 10 minutes.

---

9. Take the chicken off the grill; give it another generous dip in the BBQ sauce, and place it back on the grill for another 5 to 10 minutes.

10. Eat with grilled corn, sour-cream-and-onion potato chips, mashed potatoes, or whatever else you've got.

Note: Assuming this is a tailgate BBQ, you can bake the chicken the day of or the night before the tailgate. Also, the recipe requires a charcoal grill—none of this gas nonsense.

—Jake Tulsky
Burlington, VT (Philly born and bred)

Grilled Boneless Ribs

Ingredients

- 2 tablespoons olive oil
- 1/4 cup chopped onions
- 2 tablespoons minced garlic
- 1 cup ketchup
- 3 tablespoons Worcestershire sauce
- 1/3 cup mustard
- 1/4 cup brown sugar
- 1/2 cup apple-cider vinegar
- Tabasco sauce (a couple of drops, to taste)
- 2 pounds boneless pork ribs
- 2 tablespoons olive oil
- Salt and pepper, to taste

Directions

1. Make the sauce: In a saucepan, warm the oil over medium heat. Add the onions and garlic and cook for a couple of minutes. Add the other sauce ingredients and cook for 15 to 20 minutes, stirring often. Set aside.
2. Coat the ribs with the oil, salt, and pepper.
3. Separate the sauce into two bowls. Generously coat the ribs with sauce from one bowl during the last 5 to 10 minutes of grilling. Then use the other bowl of sauce for dipping after the ribs are cooked.
4. Grill the ribs on indirect medium-high heat (away from the flame) for 20 to 45 minutes until the pork is thoroughly cooked to an internal temperature of 180°F.

You get the ribs without the hassle of a long grill time ... the sauce is incredible and simple.

—Chuck Porter
Telford, PA

Chipotle Wings

Ingredients

- 2 cups ketchup
- 1/3 cup soy sauce
- 1 cup honey
- 1/3 cup red wine vinegar
- 1 tablespoon garlic
- 1 can chipotle peppers, minced
- 1 cup chicken stock
- 1/4 teaspoon black pepper
- 5 pounds chicken wings

Directions

Prep Cooking at Home

1. In a large bowl, combine the marinade ingredients. Add the chicken wings and marinate for 1 hour.

At the Ballpark

2. Wrap the wings in a tinfoil bag and place on a hot grill for 30 minutes.
3. Remove wings from the tinfoil bag and put directly on the grill to caramelize for 5 to 10 minutes.

—Sean McCall
Philadelphia, PA

Smoked Jalapeño Poppers

Ingredients

- 8 jalapeños
- 8 ounces cream cheese
- 1 can water chestnuts
- 4 slices bacon

Tools

- Kitchen gloves
- Sealable bag
- Toothpicks
- Rib rack
- Smoker
- Metal skewers

Directions

Prep at Home the Night Before

1. Cut off the tops of the jalapeños and remove the insides. (I recommend some kitchen gloves for this.)

2. Let the cream cheese come to room temperature and load it in the sealable bag.
3. Cut one of the corner tips off of the bag and pump each of the jalapeños half-full with cream cheese.
4. Add a water chestnut (it may need to be trimmed) to each.
5. Wrap the bacon around the jalapeños—usually half a piece works well—and secure it with the toothpick. Refrigerate overnight.

At the Ballpark

6. Stand up the rib rack in the smoker and use the skewers to secure the jalapeños upright. (See the photo for a demonstration.)
7. Smoke for two hours.

This recipe is best done in a smoker, but grilling will work as well, low and slow. The water chestnuts are a huge difference-maker in this recipe. They add a nice crunch to the jalapeños without messing with the flavor.

—Scott Grotyohann
Connecticut

Glazed and Confused

Ingredients

- 1 1/4-pound beef patty
- 4 strips bacon
- 1 egg
- 1 glazed donut, sliced
- 2 slices American cheese

Recommended Beers

- American Strong Ale, Double IPA, or Black IPA

Directions

1. Begin by cooking your hamburger and bacon as you normally would.
2. When the meat is nearly done, fry the egg.
3. When the egg is nearly done, slice the glazed donut (bun style) and place it on your grill flat side down. Keep a close eye so as not to burn, and grill until golden brown.
4. While the donut is grilling, stack the bacon and egg on the burger and top with the cheese.
5. When the cheese is melted, remove the burger from the heat and place on half of the glazed donut (remember, keep the flat grilled sides out on the donuts). Top with the other donut half.

—Joshua Lepley
Barleydine.com
Williamsport, PA

Sweet 'n' Spicy Shrimp on the Barbie

Ingredients

- 2 pounds medium to large shrimp
- 1/4 cup olive oil
- 1 1/2 tablespoons garlic, crushed or minced
- 1 tablespoon chopped cilantro
- 1 jalapeño, seeded and minced
- 1 1/2 tablespoons Sriracha (Thai hot sauce)
- 1 teaspoon salt
- 1 teaspoon honey
- 1/2 teaspoon Worcestershire sauce
- 1/2 teaspoon red pepper flakes
- Juice of 1 lime

Tools

- 4 to 6 skewers, wood (soaked in water) or metal

Directions

Prep at Home

1. Peel, devein, and clean the shrimp; set aside.
2. Mix the rest of the ingredients in a flat plastic container using a spoon.
3. Add the shrimp and close the cover.
4. Shake gently to coat the shrimp in the mixture.
5. Allow the shrimp to marinate, chilled, at least 1 hour but no more than 3 hours.

At the Ballpark

6. Prepare a hot grill and thread the shrimp onto skewers.

Put two skewers through each shrimp to make it easier to flip on the grill.

7. Place the shrimp skewers on the grill and cook for about 3 minutes on each side, or until the shrimp turn pink and are lightly charred on both sides. Do not overcook.

—Jason Lyons
Arlington, VA

Grilled Steak and Shrimp Kabobs

Ingredients

- 1 1/2 to 2 pounds lean beef (preferably filet mignon loin, although any steak cut will do)
- 1 zucchini
- 1 eggplant
- 1 green bell pepper
- 1 yellow bell pepper
- 1 red bell pepper
- 1 Spanish onion
- 1 pint cherry tomatoes
- 2 cups olive oil
- 1 clove garlic, minced
- 2 tablespoons chopped basil
- 1/2 pound medium-size shrimp, peeled and cleaned
- 1 tablespoon Old Bay Seasoning
- 2 teaspoons lemon juice (or juice of 1 lemon)
- Salt and pepper, to taste
- Lemon wedges, for garnish
- Fresh basil sprigs, for garnish

Tools

- Skewers, preferably metal

Directions

Prep at Home

1. Begin by cutting the beef into 1-inch to 1-1/2-inch cubes, or enough to place 4 on each skewer.
2. Cut the zucchini into thick slices to make round circles.

3. Peel the eggplant. Cut it into thick slices about 1 inch long and 1 inch wide.
4. Clean the peppers. Cut into square slices, about 1 inch or so wide.
5. Do the same with the onion. You want the kabobs to look uniform, so all of the pieces should be about the same size.
6. Place the beef cubes and vegetables (along with the tomatoes) into a large bowl.
7. Add 1 1/2 cups of the olive oil, 1 1/2 tablespoons of the chopped basil, half of the minced garlic, and the salt and pepper. Mix this up until the vegetables and beef cubes are covered evenly.
8. Refrigerate this mixture for at least 6 hours (24 hours is recommended).
9. Place all of the shrimp into a bowl.
10. Add the remaining olive oil, garlic, and lemon juice, and the Old Bay Seasoning.
11. Mix until the shrimp are covered evenly.
12. Refrigerate the shrimp mixture for about an hour.

At the Ballpark

13. When you are ready to grill, light your grill and let it get hot.
14. While it's getting hot, you can prep your skewers. Start off with a tomato at the top to hold everything on, and then layer the shrimp, vegetables, and beef, finishing off with a tomato at the bottom, leaving about an inch at the top and two inches at the bottom.
15. When you're ready to grill, just place the skewers across the bars to get some good grill marks close to the heat.

Turn each one every 3 to 4 minutes (a total of four times), allowing each side to brown evenly.

16. Keep an eye on the kabobs, as some of the vegetables may brown a little faster. If this happens, move the skewer to a cooler part of the grill, or the upper rack, so as to not burn the vegetables completely. You want a good amount of brown or char on the vegetables, though; it just adds to the flavor. The beef should come out about medium, though you'll probably get a variety of temperatures.

17. Garnish with a lemon wedge and a sprig of fresh basil.

Serve over white rice or rice pilaf, or over a bed of fried leeks.

—Jeff Ehrmann
ProfessionalRecipes.com
Philadelphia, PA

Laham Mishwe (Lamb on a Skewer)

Ingredients

- 2 pounds lamb, cut into cubes
- 8 small onions, cut into quarters and then separated
- 2 tablespoons olive oil
- Salt and pepper, to taste
- 8 to 12 pitas

Directions

1. On each skewer, alternate one piece of lamb, then one piece of onion, etc.
2. Brush with oil and sprinkle with salt and pepper.
3. Place on the grill and cook to your preferred healthy temperature (150°F for medium).
4. Eat while hot with Lebanese pita bread warmed on the grill, garlic dipping sauce, and salad.

This recipe is ideal for an outdoor barbecue. There are many variations depending on individual taste. We always use lamb, as this meat is not greasy, dry, or stringy. Either lamb leg or shoulder can be used. You will find the shoulder is juicier.

It's also wonderful with other vegetables, such as tomatoes or green bell peppers, which can be alternated with the meat. You can also marinate the lamb the night before by soaking it in white wine, garlic, and oregano.

—Brian's Lebanese grandmother "Siti"
Philadelphia, PA

Foil-Wrapped Bruschetta Chicken Bake

Ingredients

- 1 28-ounce can diced tomatoes, drained
- 2 cloves garlic, minced
- 1/2 loaf French bread, cut into slices, toasted, and then cut into cubes
- 2 teaspoons Italian seasoning
- 2 teaspoons dried parsley flakes
- Cooking spray
- 6 boneless, skinless chicken breasts
- 1 teaspoon dried basil leaves
- 1 to 2 cups shredded mozzarella cheese

Directions

1. In a bowl, mix the drained tomatoes, garlic, diced toasted bread, Italian seasoning, and parsley flakes until moistened.
2. Spray 6 large sheets of heavy-duty aluminum foil with cooking spray and place one chicken breast in the center of each.
3. Sprinkle the top of each breast with the dried basil leaves, and then top with the bread-and-tomato mixture followed by a sprinkling of mozzarella.
4. Double-fold the sides and top of each packet, leaving room for steam. Keep refrigerated until time for grilling (either at home or at the ballpark).
5. Once the grill is hot, place the foil packets in a foil tray or upper rack. Leave covered for 30 to 35 minutes or until the chicken achieves an internal temperature of 165°F.

6. Let cool for 5 minutes, and be careful of steam when opening.

—George Keiper
Bristol, PA

Spicy Bacon-Wrapped BBQ Shrimp

Ingredients

- Extra-large uncooked jumbo shrimp (cleaned, deveined, with tails on)
- Uncooked hickory-smoked bacon, cut into thirds (one third for each shrimp)
- Barbecue sauce
- Pinch of cinnamon and sugar

Tools

- Toothpicks

Directions

1. Preheat your grill.
2. Wrap each shrimp with bacon and secure with a toothpick.
3. Baste with barbecue sauce on each side and place directly on the grill (the bacon grease will keep them from sticking, but be careful of flare-ups). These tasty treats need about 4 minutes per side.
4. Dust with cinnamon and sugar

I made these tasty treats during a tailgating cookout I had recently. After the first bite, we fell in love with them; they were perfect tailgating fare! The trick will be to prep them the night before so you're not handing raw bacon at the tailgate. Enjoy!

—Colin Richards
Destin, FL

Hot Dog Road Trip!

There's nothing quite like a hot dog cooked over an open flame to get you ready for a baseball game. If you're following the Phils on a road trip around America, there's a chance you'll run into one of these regional hot dog variations.

New York: A beef hot dog boiled or cooked on a griddle, and then topped with mustard, sauerkraut, and sweet red onions.

DC Half Smoke: A large spicy steamed sausage—either a pork and beef mix or all-beef—on a steamed bun. Some places will load it up with chili, mustard, and chopped raw onions.

Chicago Dog: An all-beef dog in a steamed poppy-seed bun with yellow mustard, chopped white onion, neon sweet pickle relish, sport peppers, pickle spear, halved tomato slices, and celery salt.

Midwest Coney Dog: Coneys are small all-beef natural-casing dogs served in steamed buns and topped with minced-meat chili, mustard, and chopped onions (serving one "loaded" means adding shredded cheddar).

Texas: A beef frank served with chili sauce (actually made famous in Altoona, Pennsylvania, and Paterson, New Jersey).

Phoenix Sonoran: A beef frank wrapped in bacon and then cooked on a griddle and piled with pinto beans, grilled onions, chopped tomatoes, mayonnaise or sour cream, mustard, and salsa verde.

Dodger Dog: Featured at Dodger Stadium, these are skinless

foot-long pork hot dogs in a steamed bun. You can get the dogs steamed or grilled.

South Philly: Served at Citizens Bank Park and winner of its hot-dog contest, it's a grilled hot dog with broccoli rabe, roasted long hot peppers, and shaved sharp provolone on seeded Italian bread.

Phillies Nation Dog: A favorite at our tailgates, this is a beef hot dog sliced open lengthwise, stuffed with jalapeno slices and cheddar cheese, wrapped in bacon, and then grilled until crispy.

—Brian Michael

At Home

Only a handful of the most diehard fans can make it to every Phillies game. For the rest of us, there are plenty of opportunities to enjoy game-day food at home while you watch the contest on TV, listen to it on the radio, or stream it over the Internet. Most recipes can be made either on the grill or in the kitchen, so you'll be prepared no matter what the weather is like.

Good Dog Burger

Ingredients

- 1 tablespoon unsalted butter
- 1 tablespoon olive oil
- 1 pound Spanish onions, sliced thin
- Kosher salt and black pepper, as needed
- 1 tablespoon chopped fresh thyme leaves
- 2 pounds 80/20 blend ground sirloin
- 4 ounces Roquefort cheese, divided into 4 equal chunks
- 4 brioche burger buns

Directions

For the Onions

1. In a sauté pan over medium-high heat, combine the butter and oil.
2. When the butter is melted, add the onions to the pan, stirring to coat.
3. Season with salt and pepper.
4. Let sit until the onions start to brown, about 20 minutes.
5. Stir again and add the thyme.
6. Reduce heat to low and simmer until the liquid released by the onions is reduced to almost dry and the onions are caramelized.

For the Burgers

1. Loosely roll the ground beef into 4 8-ounce balls.
2. Pat each ball into a flat patty, and place a 1 oz. chunk of Roquefort cheese in the center of each one.
3. Gently fold the edges of each patty up around the cheese and roll it back into a ball so that the cheese stays in the center of the ball.
4. Gently flatten the ball into a hamburger shape, about 5 inches across by 1 inch thick.
5. Season generously with salt and pepper.
6. Grill about 6 minutes per side (for medium).
7. Cut a roll in half. Place a burger on the bottom half. Top with caramelized onions and the top of the bun. Repeat for remaining rolls and burgers.

Serve with fries or your favorite side dish.

—Jessica O'Donnell
Good Dog Bar
224 South Fifteenth Street
Philadelphia, PA

Chicken Satay with Cucumber Salad

Cucumber Salad

Ingredients

- 3 cups red wine vinegar
- 1/2 cup honey
- 1 cucumber
- 5 baby carrots
- 1 red onion
- 1 jalapeño
- 1 red or green bell pepper
- 1 teaspoon cilantro, chopped
- Pinch of salt

Directions

1. Boil red wine vinegar and honey for 10 minutes. Allow the dressing to cool.
2. Cut the cucumber in half and remove seeds.
3. Slice the cucumber into half-moon shapes.
4. Cut the carrots into thin circles.
5. Slice the red onion into thin strips.
6. Slice the pepper into thin strips
7. Cut the jalapeños in half, remove seeds, and then slice into thin strips.
8. Add the dressing and cilantro to the salad and refrigerate for at least 2 hours.

Chicken Satay

Ingredients

- 5 cloves garlic, roasted and diced
- 4 tablespoons curry powder

- 2 tablespoons ginger root, grated
- 16 ounces Greek or plain yogurt
- 3 tablespoons olive oil
- 8 boneless chicken breasts, butterflied and tenderized
- Cucumber Salad (above)
- Parsley, chopped for garnish

Tools

- 40 6-inch wooden skewers

Directions

1. Mix together roasted garlic, curry, grated ginger root, yogurt, and oil.
2. Place mixture in a tall container.
3. Soak the skewers in water for 10 minutes to prevent burning on the grill.
4. Cut the chicken into 1/2-inch-thick strips.
5. Skewer the chicken lengthwise.
6. Add the chicken to the marinade in the tall container and marinate at least 1 hour before cooking.
7. Grill the chicken skewers 1 minute on each side.
8. Bake in a 350ºF oven for 10 minutes.
9. Place the Cucumber Salad in the center of a plate.
10. Arrange the chicken satay skewers pointing toward center of plate around the salad and sprinkle with the chopped parsley.

—Scott Auslander
Ventnor Sports Cafe
2411 Eighteenth Street, NW
Washington, DC

Crab Rangoon

Ingredients

- 3/4 quart vegetable or canola oil
- 12 ounces cream cheese, at room temperature
- 1 cup imitation crabmeat
- 2 green onions, minced
- 1/4 teaspoon garlic powder
- 1/2 teaspoon soy sauce
- 1 egg, beaten
- 1 package wonton wrappers
- Sweet-and-sour sauce, for serving

Directions

1. Preheat oil in a pot to 375°F.
2. Combine cream cheese, crabmeat, onions, garlic powder, and soy sauce.
3. Beat the egg and a little water to make egg wash.
4. Brush the opposite corners of a wonton wrapper with the egg mixture. Add filling to the center of the wonton and fold over the edges of the wrapper to form a triangle. Seal tightly. (A trick I like to use is to take a fork and press the edges of the wonton to give it an even better seal, and it also creates a nice presentation.)
5. Brush wontons with egg wash and deep-fry in oil for 2 to 3 minutes until golden brown.
6. Serve with a side of sweet-and-sour sauce.

—Kelli Amato
Phoenixville, PA

Grand Salami Pie

Ingredients

- 1 package crescent rolls
- 3 eggs, beaten
- 1 pound mozzarella cheese, grated
- 1/2 to 3/4 pound hard salami, chopped
- 3 tablespoons Parmesan cheese, grated

Directions

1. Press the crescent rolls into an ungreased 9-by-13-inch glass baking dish.
2. Press seams closed.
3. In a mixing bowl, beat the eggs.
4. Add mozzarella cheese, salami, and Parmesan cheese, and mix until well blended.
5. Spread the mixture over crescent rolls and bake at 300°F for 35 to 40 minutes.
6. Cool to room temperature.
7. Cut into squares.
8. Go Phillies!

—Michael and Holly Roth
Northampton, PA

Beef Stew for a Crowd

Ingredients

- 1 cup Italian salad dressing
- 3 to 4 pounds beef cubes (for stewing)
- 1 pound bacon, chopped
- 1 large yellow onion, chopped
- 1/2 teaspoon celery seeds
- Healthy sprinkle of garlic powder
- Healthy sprinkle of onion powder
- Salt and pepper, to taste
- 5 to 6 medium-size carrots, chopped
- 4 pounds potatoes, peeled and chopped
- 1 32-ounce can stewed tomatoes with Italian seasonings, undrained
- 1 32-ounce can beef broth
- 2 14-ounce cans beef gravy with onions

Directions

1. Pour dressing over the beef cubes and let marinate for at least an hour.
2. Cook the bacon in a large heavy-bottom pot until crisp; reserve fat.
3. Add onions and sauté in bacon fat until clear, about 4 minutes.
4. Add the beef cubes (discard marinade) and seasonings (celery seeds, garlic powder, onion powder, salt, and pepper) and cook until the beef is browned.
5. Add the remaining ingredients and cook on medium-high until the stew comes to a boil.
6. Once boiling, turn the heat down to low and cook covered for 3 to 4 hours, stirring every so often.

7. This stew tastes even better the next day, so make it the night before and then reheat 1/2 hour before you're ready to eat.
8. Go Phillies!

—Dori
Essington, PA

The Food Insulter's Chili Recipe

Ingredients

- 2 medium onions, diced
- 4 large cloves garlic, minced
- 4 teaspoons vegetable oil, for sautéing
- 1 pound 80/20 blend ground beef
- 1/2 pound boneless pork rib
- 1 teaspoon kosher salt
- 1/2 teaspoon black pepper
- 2 or 3 chili peppers, diced
- 3 or 4 tablespoons chili powder
- 1 tablespoon cumin
- 1 teaspoon cayenne
- 1 teaspoon coriander
- 1 teaspoon paprika
- 1 teaspoon cinnamon
- 1 teaspoon oregano
- 1/2 teaspoon garlic powder
- 1 16-ounce can red beans, drained
- 1 16-ounce can black beans, drained
- 2 14-1/2-ounce cans diced tomatoes (do not drain)
- 1 dash liquid smoke

Directions

1. Dice the onions and sauté with the garlic and oil in a pan over medium heat, about 5 to 10 minutes.
2. Cut the pork into strips 1 to 2 inches in length.
3. Season the beef and pork with the salt and pepper. Add to the pan and cook on medium heat until browned.
4. Add the chili peppers.

5. Mix all of the spices together in a bowl, and then add to the pan.
6. Add the beans.
7. Add the tomatoes.
8. Add the liquid smoke.
9. Cook on low for 1 to 2 hours.

—Jake Tulsky
Burlington, VT (Philly born and bred)

Quick and Easy Smoky Corn Chowder

Ingredients

- 1 large onion, chopped
- 1 tablespoon vegetable oil, for sautéing
- 1 pound ham steak (1/2 inch thick), diced
- 2 cans whole kernel corn (do not drain)
- 2 cans whole canned potatoes, chopped
- 2 cans creamed corn
- 2 cans condensed cream of chicken soup
- Healthy dash of bacon bits
- 1 can condensed chicken rice soup
- Salt and pepper, to taste
- 2 cups shredded cheddar cheese

Directions

1. Sauté onions in a pot with a small amount of oil until they are soft.
2. Add diced ham and cook for 5 minutes.
3. Add remaining ingredients, except cheese.
4. Cook on low heat for 2 to 3 hours.
5. Remove from heat and sprinkle with cheese.

This soup tastes better the next day, so make it the night before the big game. Just heat through and enjoy!

Go Phillies!

—Dori
Essington, PA

Slow-Cooker Cuban Braised Beef and Peppers

Ingredients

- 1 28-ounce can diced tomatoes, drained
- 2 red bell peppers, sliced 1/2 inch thick
- 1 onion, cut into 8 wedges
- 2 teaspoons dried oregano
- 1 teaspoon ground cumin
- Kosher salt and black pepper
- 1 1/2 pounds flank steak, cut crosswise into thirds
- 1 cup long-grain white rice
- 1 avocado, sliced
- 1/4 cup fresh cilantro leaves

Directions

1. In a 5- to 6-quart slow cooker, combine the tomatoes, bell peppers, onion, oregano, cumin, 1 1/2 teaspoons salt, and 1/4 teaspoon pepper. Nestle the steak among the vegetables.
2. Cook, covered, until the meat is tender and pulls apart easily, on high for 4 to 5 hours or on low for 7 to 8 hours.
3. About 25 minutes before serving, cook the rice according to the package directions.
4. Using two forks, shred the beef and mix it into the cooking liquid.
5. Serve with the rice and top with the avocado and cilantro.

—Kelli Amato
Phoenixville, PA

Three-Meat Gadunk

Ingredients

- 1 pound ground beef
- 1 16-ounce pack Neese's spicy sausage (it's a block of sausage)
- 1 pack Johnsonville Italian sausage
- 1 15-ounce can black beans, drained
- 1 15-ounce can chili beans, drained
- 1 15-ounce can red kidney beans, drained
- 1 15-ounce can RO*TEL tomatoes and green peppers (mild or hot), drained
- 1 15-ounce can diced tomatoes, drained
- 1 45-ounce jar Ragú traditional spaghetti sauce
- 5 medium sweet onions, diced
- 1 bottle beer
- 2 cups red wine vinegar
- 1 cup brown sugar
- Hot sauce or chili powder
- Sour cream, for serving
- Grated cheese, for serving
- Cornbread or other bread for dipping

Directions

1. Brown the ground beef in a pan over medium heat and drain.
2. Brown the spicy sausage and drain.
3. Cut up all of the Italian sausages into slices, brown, and drain.
4. Add all the meat to a chili pot.
5. Add the beans to the chili pot.
6. Add the can of RO*TEL and the can of diced tomatoes.

7. Add the spaghetti sauce.
8. Add the diced onions.
9. Add the beer.
10. Add the red wine vinegar.
11. Add the brown sugar.
12. Add as much hot sauce as you want and stir.
13. Allow to simmer on low to medium heat for 1 to 2 hours.
14. Serve with sour cream, grated cheese, and bread.

—Gavin Fisher
Spartanburg, SC

Barleydine Breakfast Sandwich

Ingredients

- 4 ounces sirloin steak
- 8 to 12 french fries
- 1 slice pepper jack cheese
- 1 slice American cheese
- 1 slice sharp cheddar
- 2 ounces taco cheese
- 1 Italian hoagie roll
- 2 eggs, fried

Recommended Beers

- Lancaster Brewing Company Milk Stout or Yards Love Stout

Directions

1. Begin by grilling the steak and preparing the fries. This is actually a perfect sandwich to use up some leftovers from dinner the night before.
2. Once the steak is ready, place cheese on the roll and layer with the steak.
3. Top with a layer of cheese and add fries with another layer of cheese.
4. Eggs are last, with yet another layer of cheese.
5. Pop the sandwich in the broiler until the roll begins to turn brown.
6. Remove, let stand for several minutes, and eat. Enjoy!

Without a doubt the best breakfast sandwich I have ever eaten.

—Joshua Lepley
Barleydine.com
Williamsport, PA

Crawfish Crab Cakes

Ingredients

- 2 medium onions, diced
- 2 tablespoons garlic, minced
- 1 pound cooked crawfish tail meat, diced
- 1 pound pasteurized back fin crabmeat, drained
- 1 1/4 cups mayonnaise
- 1/4 cup spicy brown mustard
- 1/4 cup fresh parsley, chopped
- 3/4 cup panko bread crumbs
- 3 tablespoons Old Bay Seasoning
- 1 tablespoons kosher salt
- 1 1/2 teaspoons ground black pepper
- 5 ounces vegetable or olive oil for pan frying

Directions

1. Heat 3 tablespoons of oil in frying pan over medium-high heat.
2. Sauté onions and garlic until onions appear translucent (approximately 12 minutes). Put aside to cool.
3. Combine remaining ingredients in large mixing bowl and fold together.
4. Add cooled onions and garlic and fold until well combined.
5. Shape mixture into 6-ounce patties (approximately 1 inch thick). Chill in refrigerator (or cooler) for at least 1 hour.
6. Preheat oven (or grill) to 425°F.
7. Heat 2 tablespoons of oil in a medium frying pan over medium-high heat.
8. Cook patties until golden brown on both sides (approximately 3 minutes per side).

9. Bake at 425°F for 5 minutes (or place on top rack of grill).

10. Add your favorite greens and serve on a toasted bun, over salad, or enjoy the cake on its own. Recommended condiments include cocktail sauce, tartar sauce, spicy aioli, or hot sauce. Makes approximately 8–10 cakes.

—David Champagne
The Grey Lodge Public House
6235 Frankford Avenue
Philadelphia, PA

Southwestern Short Ribs in a Dutch Oven

Ingredients

- 6 pounds beef short ribs
- 1 tablespoon salt
- 2 tablespoons ground pepper
- 1 tablespoon garlic powder
- 2 medium onions, diced
- 2 tablespoons chopped garlic
- 1/4 cup balsamic vinegar
- 1/4 cup Worcestershire sauce
- 2 tablespoons dark mustard
- 3 cups of your favorite barbeque sauce (or make your own with 1 can tomato sauce, 1 small can tomato paste, and 3/4 cup brown sugar)

Tools

- Dutch oven pot

Directions

1. Remove the back casing from the ribs.
2. Season the ribs with salt, pepper, and garlic powder.
3. Braise the ribs in the Dutch oven and then remove from the pot.
4. Sauté the onions in the Dutch oven.
5. Add all other ingredients and cook for 20 minutes.
6. Preheat oven to 325ºF.
7. Remove 3/4 of the sauce from the Dutch oven and reserve.
8. Add the ribs back into the Dutch oven.
9. Pour the reserved sauce over the top of the ribs.
10. Bake on 325ºF for 2 hours.

—Sandra Michael
Philadelphia, PA

Tabouli (Middle Eastern Salsa)

Ingredients

- 1 cup medium bulgur (cracked wheat)
- 4 ripe medium-size tomatoes, chopped into small cubes
- 4 or 5 spring onions (with the green parts), chopped into 1/4-inch lengths
- Salt and pepper
- 1/2 teaspoon allspice
- 1/2 cup lemon juice
- 5 tablespoons good olive oil
- 1/2 cup finely chopped fresh mint
- 3 cups finely chopped flat-leaf parsley leaves
- Romaine lettuce leaves, for serving

Directions

1. Rinse the bulgur several times and then soak in cold water for about 20 minutes. Put in a sieve to drain.
2. Put the bulgur, tomato, and onion in a large mixing or serving bowl. Add salt, pepper, allspice, lemon juice, olive oil, mint, and parsley.
3. Taste for seasoning. If too dry, you can add additional lemon juice.
4. Toss well. Tabouli benefits from resting—you can cover the bowl with plastic wrap and leave in the refrigerator for a few hours or overnight, tossing occasionally.
5. Serve with romaine lettuce leaves. Scoop some tabouli into a leaf and enjoy!

—Amin Bitar
Bitar's Lebanese Restaurant
947 Federal Street
Philadelphia, PA

Tex-Mex Veggie Pizza Squares

Ingredients

- 1 8-ounce package refrigerated crescent rolls
- 1 8-ounce package cream cheese, softened
- 1/2 1-ounce package taco seasoning mix
- 1 8-ounce package shredded Mexican cheese
- Veggies of your choice, cut into small pieces
  1/2 cup tomatoes
  1/2 cup red bell pepper
  1/2 cup green bell pepper
  1/2 cup black olives
  1/4 cup chopped scallions

Directions

1. Preheat oven to 375ºF.
2. Roll out the crescent dough onto a large nonstick baking sheet. Stretch and flatten to form a single rectangular shape on the baking sheet.
3. Bake 11 to 13 minutes, or until golden brown. Allow to cool.
4. Place cream cheese in a medium bowl and mix with the taco seasoning mix. Adjust amount to taste. Spread mixture over cooled crust.
5. Spread the package of shredded cheese over top of cream cheese mixture.
6. Arrange veggies on top and chill for 1 hour.
7. Cut into bite-size squares to serve.

—Kelli Amato
Phoenixville, PA

My Famous Mac and Cheese

Ingredients

Macaroni

- 1/2 pound elbow macaroni
- 3 tablespoons butter
- 3 tablespoons flour
- 1 tablespoon powdered mustard
- 3 cups milk
- 1/2 cup yellow onion, finely diced
- 1 bay leaf
- 1/2 teaspoon paprika
- 1 large egg
- 12 ounces shredded sharp cheddar
- 1 teaspoon kosher salt
- Fresh black pepper

Topping

- 3 tablespoons butter
- 1 cup bread crumbs

Directions

1. Preheat oven to 350°F.
2. In a large pot of boiling, salted water, cook the pasta to al dente, about 5 minutes. Drain and set aside.
3. In a separate pot, melt the butter.
4. Whisk the flour and mustard in with the butter and keep it moving for about 5 minutes. Make sure it's free of lumps.
5. Stir in the milk, onion, bay leaf, and paprika.
6. Simmer for 10 minutes and remove the bay leaf.

7. Add in the egg.
8. Stir in 3/4 of the cheese.
9. Season with salt and pepper.
10. Fold the macaroni into the mix.
11. Pour into a 2-quart casserole dish and top with the remaining cheese.
12. Make the topping: Melt the butter in a sauté pan. Toss the bread crumbs to coat.
13. Top the macaroni with the crumb mixture and bake in the oven for 30 minutes.
14. Remove from the oven and allow the dish to rest for 5 minutes before serving.

Remember to save leftovers for fried macaroni and cheese!

—Kelli Amato
Phoenixville, PA

Philly Cheesesteak Spring Rolls with Spicy Ranch Dipping Sauce

Spring Rolls

Ingredients

- 2 cups canola or vegetable oil
- 1/2 medium yellow onion, diced
- 8 ounces 94-percent fat-free sirloin tip beef steaks (Landis is recommended, but Steak-umms work too)
- Salt and pepper, to taste
- 12 spring-roll wrappers
- 1/8 pound white American cheese, thinly sliced

Directions

1. Heat 1 1/2 tablespoons of the canola oil in a pan and sauté the onion over medium heat for 4 minutes.

2. Add the entire package of steaks (the meat can be frozen).

3. Allow the steaks to soften and begin to tear them apart using a wooden spoon and fork. The meat should be finely chopped. Add salt and pepper.

4. When all the meat is browned, remove the pan from the heat and strain the meat and onions to remove any excess liquid.

5. Once the filling is drained, it is time to assemble the rolls. Separate a single wrapper and place it so it is shaped like a diamond in front of you. Break off a piece of cheese about 2 inches by 1/2 inch and place it just below the center of the wrapper. Add about 2 tablespoons of steak and onions, and then place another small piece of cheese on top. To wrap the roll, fold the corner closest to you up to the center of the wrapper and make sure it is tight against the filling. Then fold in the right and left corners. Next, roll the wrapped mixture up to the top corner, but before rolling it all the way, moisten the top corner with a few drops of water—this will help keep the roll sealed. Repeat this process until all the filling has been used.

6. Heat the remaining oil (just under 2 cups) in a large saucepan over medium-high heat for 5 minutes. If you have a deep fryer, you can use that instead. (This would be a good time to make the dipping sauce—see below.)

7. Place as many spring rolls into the oil as you can while still allowing an inch of separation between them.

8. Rotate the spring rolls every 1 to 2 minutes on each of their four sides until they have a golden-brown color.

9. Remove the spring rolls from the pan and allow them to cool on a wire rack for 5 minutes.

10. Slice each spring roll in half on a diagonal and serve with Spicy Ranch Dipping Sauce.

Spicy Ranch Dipping Sauce

Ingredients

- 4 ounces ranch dressing
- 2 ounces buffalo sauce

Directions

1. Combine the ranch dressing and buffalo sauce in a bowl and mix with a fork or small whisk.
2. Serve slightly chilled.

—Brian Michael
Philadelphia, PA

Loaded-Baked-Potato Soup

Ingredients

- 4 baking potatoes, about 2 1/2 pounds
- 2 tablespoons butter
- 1/4 large onion, chopped
- 1 clove garlic, minced
- 2/3 cup all-purpose flour, about 3 ounces
- 6 cups milk (use 2 percent reduced fat if you prefer)
- 4 ounces shredded extra-sharp cheddar cheese, divided (use reduced fat if you prefer)
- 1 teaspoon salt
- 1/2 teaspoon freshly ground black pepper
- 1 cup reduced-fat sour cream
- 3/4 cup chopped green onions, divided
- 6 bacon slices, cooked and crumbled
- Cracked black pepper (optional)

Directions

1. Preheat oven to 400°F.
2. Pierce the potatoes with a fork. Bake at 400ºF for 1 hour, or until tender. Cool. Peel potatoes and coarsely mash.
3. In a large pot or Dutch oven, melt the butter over medium heat. Add the onion and garlic and sauté until soft, about 8 minutes.
4. Lightly spoon flour into dry measuring cups; level with a knife. Place flour into the onion mixture and gradually add milk, stirring with a whisk until blended. Cook over medium heat until thick and bubbly (about 8 minutes).

5. Add the mashed potatoes, 3/4 cup of the cheese, and the salt and pepper, stirring until the cheese melts. Remove from the heat.

6. Stir in sour cream and 1/2 cup of the green onions. Cook over low heat 10 minutes or until thoroughly heated (do not boil).

7. Ladle 1 1/2 cups of soup into each of 8 bowls. Sprinkle each serving with 1 1/2 teaspoons cheese, 1 1/2 teaspoons onions, and about 1 tablespoon bacon. Garnish with cracked pepper, if desired.

—Kelli Amato
Phoenixville, PA

Crabby Cheese Fries

Ingredients

- 1 28-ounce package frozen french fries, or 5 potatoes' worth of homemade fries
- 2 cups milk
- 1 tablespoon Worcestershire sauce
- 2 teaspoons ground dry mustard
- 1 clove garlic, peeled and crushed
- 3 tablespoons all-purpose flour
- 5 cups shredded cheddar cheese
- Old Bay Seasoning, to taste
- 1 8- to 10-ounce package crabmeat

Directions

1. Cook the french fries.
2. In a medium saucepan over low heat, mix together the milk, Worcestershire sauce, dry mustard, garlic, and flour. Heat until almost boiling.
3. Gradually stir in the cheddar cheese. Continue heating until all of the cheese has melted.
4. Add the Old Bay Seasoning and crabmeat. Stir until everything is mixed with the cheese.
5. Keep the mixture warm and either pour directly on the french fries or in a serving dip bowl (or a fondue bowl, if you have it).

—Kelli Amato
Phoenixville, PA

Cooking with Booze

Whether cooking in the kitchen or in front of a grill, there should always be a drink within arm's reach. Sometimes it's to cool off the cook; however, on these occasions, we're going to use it to cook. The following chapter features recipes that incorporate alcoholic beverages. Eat and drink responsibly!

Philly Phanatic Honeydew-Melon Daiquiris

Ingredients

- 4 shots Bacardi light rum
- 3 shots Midori honeydew-melon liqueur
- 1/4 honeydew melon
- 1/2 can frozen piña colada daiquiri mixer

Directions

1. Add all of the ingredients to a blender filled with chopped ice.
2. Blend until smooth.
3. Plop a straw into this delightfully green concoction and enjoy.

There is no better daiquiri anywhere.

—Robert O'Connor
Sewell, NJ

Grilled Bratwurst with Spicy Sauerkraut in Beer

Ingredients

- 1 onion, sliced
- 1 red bell pepper, sliced
- 1 green bell pepper, sliced
- 4 jalapeños, sliced
- 3 tablespoons butter
- 1 tablespoon salt
- 1 teaspoon black pepper
- 1 can sauerkraut
- 4 cloves garlic, sliced
- 2 cans of your favorite beer
- 12 of your favorite bratwurst or kielbasa
- 1 teaspoon cayenne pepper
- 2 tablespoons Tabasco or other hot sauce
- 12 hoagie rolls
- Spicy mustard, for serving

Tools

- Dutch oven pot

Directions

1. Using a Dutch oven or other large pot safe for baking, cook the onion, peppers, and jalapeños in the butter until soft.
2. Add the salt and pepper.
3. Add the sauerkraut, garlic, beer, sausages, cayenne pepper, and hot sauce.
4. Put a lid on the pot and place in a 300°F oven for 1 hour.
5. Remove and let cool.

6. Fire up your grill and cook the sausages while you reheat the sauerkraut.
7. Place sausages on a roll and top with the sauerkraut and peppers and your favorite spicy mustard.

—Jeremy Nolen
Brauhaus Schmitz
718 South Street
Philadelphia, PA

Beer-Basted Chicken

Ingredients

- 6 bottles beer (best if you use a hoppy type of beer, such as HopDevil)
- 1 cup dry rub (store-bought or your own made with 1 tablespoon rubbed sage, 1 tablespoon garlic powder, 3 tablespoons ground black pepper, 1 tablespoon salt, 1 tablespoon mustard powder, 1 tablespoon chili powder, 1 tablespoon ground cumin, 4 tablespoons ground paprika, 1 tablespoon powdered onion)
- 10 ounces honey
- 2 medium-size chickens (parted)

Directions

1. Preheat your grill to medium-high.
2. In a saucepan, pour 2 of the bottles of beer, and then stir in the dry rub and the honey.
3. Over low heat, slowly simmer the mixture until the glaze thickens. (Hint: you can add flour or baking powder to hasten thickening.)
4. Let the sauce cool. As the sauce cools, open the third bottle of beer and consume said beer.
5. In a large sealable plastic bag, place the chicken parts. Pour in the glaze and coat the chicken. Zip the bag closed and shake.
6. Let marinate for a bit. (Now is time to drink the fourth bottle of beer.)
7. Remove the chicken from the bag and place it on the grill.
8. Coat the chicken occasionally as needed and cook for

8 minutes per side. (Time to pop open the fifth bottle of beer.)

9. Now your chicken should be a nice golden brown, so serve it up. Open that last bottle of beer and drink to your success as a grill master.

This can be prepared beforehand and stored for game day.

—Kevin Kimartin
Philadelphia, PA

Shorty's Honey Chipotle Steak

Chipotle Sauce

Ingredients

- 1/4 7-ounce can chipotle peppers in adobo sauce (more peppers = spicier)
- 4 garlic cloves
- 1 28-ounce can diced tomato
- 3 tablespoons honey
- 1/4 cup parsley
- 1/2 cup cilantro
- 1/2 cup Marsala wine

Directions

1. Place all ingredients in a food processor and blend.

Shorty's Cheesesteak

Ingredients

- 4 large Spanish onions
- Salt and pepper, to taste
- 2 tablespoons olive oil, for sautéing
- 4 8-ounce portions thinly sliced sirloin (wafer thin)
- 12 slices pepper jack cheese
- 4 9-inch hoagie rolls (must be crusty on the outside and soft on the inside)

Directions

1. Chop onions, add salt and pepper, and sauté in a pan with olive oil until caramelized.
2. Lightly oil a flat griddle and add portions of sirloin, seasoning meat with salt and pepper.

3. Spread apart steak as it cooks. (Shorty's does not chop the meat—we rough-chop it or separate it.)
4. Flip meat until it is cooked through entirely.
5. Pour 4 tablespoons of the Chipotle Sauce over each portion of meat.
6. Add 3 slices of cheese to each portion and wait for it to melt.
7. Gently fold meat into rolls and add desired amount of caramelized onions.

—Evan Stein
Shorty's 576 Ninth Avenue
(between Forty-First and Forty-Second Streets)
New York, NY

Louisiana Sausage Gumbo

Base Ingredients

- 1 cup vegetable oil
- 1 cup all-purpose baking flour
- 2 tablespoons vegetable oil
- 2 medium to large bell peppers (any color), chopped
- 1 large white or red onion, chopped
- 3 cloves garlic, minced
- 1 32-ounce carton chicken broth
- 1 pound sausage (Andouille or jerk sausage is preferred, but regular sausage is acceptable), sliced
- 3 bay leaves
- Cajun spices
- 1 16-ounce bag frozen okra
- 2 15.25-ounce cans whole kernel corn or equivalent in frozen whole kernel corn (white or yellow are both acceptable), undrained
- 1 28-ounce can petite diced tomatoes, drained

Optional Ingredients

- 2 long hot peppers, sliced, with seeds retained
- 1 pound other meats
- Red wine or red cooking wine (sherry, Marsala, etc. can be used)
- 1 pound shrimp, peeled, deveined, and cleaned
- Rice (yellow, Spanish, or white rice are all acceptable)
- 2 to 4 stalks celery, sliced
- Onion powder
- Hot cayenne pepper powder
- Liquid smoke
- Worcestershire sauce

- Hot pepper sauce
- Hot sauce
- Filé powder (very hard to find in the Northeast; try the Italian Market or Reading Terminal)

Tools

- Medium saucepan without Teflon
- Wooden utensils
- Metal sauce spoon
- 16-ounce jar with lid
- 5-quart stockpot without Teflon (cast iron, if possible)
- Soup ladle

Directions

1. Make the roux: In a medium saucepan, heat the vegetable oil over low heat. Once the oil is hot, slowly add in 1 cup of flour and mix slowly with a wooden spatula. Once the mixture gets to a chocolate-brown color (10 to 15 minutes), remove from the stove and wait for 5 minutes for the roux to cool. You may choose to cook the roux longer for more flavor, but be extremely careful not to burn the mixture. Afterward, use a metal sauce spoon to put all the roux in a clean 16-ounce jar. Roux can be kept in a sealed jar for approximately 6 months in the refrigerator.
2. Place 2 tablespoons of vegetable oil in the stockpot.
3. Cook the bell peppers, onions, garlic, and long hot peppers (optional) until tender, approximately 5 to 7 minutes.
4. Add 2 to 3 tablespoons of roux to the onion mixture and mix thoroughly.

5. Add the chicken broth all at once and bring to a boil. It should begin thickening.
6. Add the sausage (and/or other meats), bay leaves, and spices. If you wish, you can add 1/2 to 1 cup of red (cooking) wine at this point.
7. Reduce heat and allow to simmer for 15 minutes, mixing occasionally.
8. Add 1/2 of the bag of frozen okra, both cans of whole kernel corn, and the entire can of petite diced tomatoes.
9. Allow to simmer for another 15 minutes, mixing occasionally.
10. If you wish to add shrimp, add during the last 5 minutes of cooking. Do not overcook the shrimp!
11. Remove from heat, allow to cool, and remove bay leaves.
12. Add filé powder and hot sauce and serve over rice, if you wish.

Louisiana gumbo is essentially the southern equivalent of New England clam chowder, a soup "casserole" in its tradition. This recipe is very versatile, but the base ingredients listed above should not be changed. If you choose to add more meat or add shrimp, I suggest using about 1 pound of each and a slightly bigger stockpot from which to cook. Bear in mind you do have flexibility in the optional ingredients and can remove or supplement, as you wish.

—Andrew Wong
Philadelphia, PA

Sausage and Peppers

Ingredients

- 1/4 cup extra-virgin olive oil
- 1 pound sweet Italian turkey or pork sausage
- 2 red bell peppers, sliced
- 2 yellow onions, sliced
- 1 teaspoon kosher salt
- 1 teaspoon freshly ground black pepper
- 1/2 teaspoon dried oregano
- 1/2 cup chopped fresh basil leaves
- 4 garlic cloves, chopped
- 2 tablespoons tomato paste
- 1 cup Marsala wine
- 1 15-ounce can diced tomatoes
- 1/4 teaspoon red pepper flakes, optional
- 4 to 6 fresh Italian sandwich rolls, optional

Directions

1. Heat the oil in a heavy large skillet over medium heat.
2. Add the sausages and cook until brown on both sides, about 7 to 10 minutes.
3. Remove from the pan and drain.
4. Keeping the pan over medium heat, add the peppers, onions, salt, and pepper. Cook until golden brown, about 5 minutes.
5. Add the oregano, basil, and garlic and cook 2 more minutes.
6. Add the tomato paste and stir.
7. Add the Marsala, tomatoes, and red pepper flakes (optional). Stir to combine, scraping the bottom of the

pan with a wooden spoon to release all the browned bits.

8. Bring to a simmer.
9. Cut the sausages into 6 pieces each, about 1-inch cubes.
10. Add the sausage back to the pan and stir to combine. Cook until the sauce has thickened, about 20 minutes.
11. Serve in bowls or, if serving as a sandwich, split the rolls in half lengthwise. Hollow out the bread from the bottom side of each roll, being careful not to puncture the crust. Toast the rolls and then fill the bottom half of each with the sausage mixture. Top with the other half of the roll and serve the sandwiches immediately.

—Kelli Amato
Phoenixville, PA

"You Won't Miss the Butter" King Crab Legs

Ingredients

- 5 pounds king crab legs
- 1 bunch cilantro, chopped (leaf only)
- 1 bunch basil, chopped
- 5 cloves minced garlic
- 6 Roma tomatoes, chopped
- 2 tablespoons Old Bay Seasoning
- Half a 1.5-liter bottle Sauvignon Blanc
- 1/2 red onion, chopped
- 1/2 Spanish onion, chopped
- 1 red bell pepper, chopped
- 1 stick butter
- 2 tablespoons kosher salt
- 2 tablespoons whole black peppercorns

Directions

1. Place all of the ingredients in a pot and bring to a boil.
2. Let boil uncovered for 2 minutes.
3. Cover and continue to boil for 10 minutes.
4. Remove crab legs and place into a serving bowl.
5. Allow the liquid to boil for 2 additional minutes and then pour over crab legs.

—Joshua Lepley
Barleydine.com
Williamsport, PA

Breckenridge Brewery Vanilla Porter Milkshake

Ingredients

- 4 scoops plain vanilla ice cream
- 1/2 bottle Breckenridge Brewery Vanilla Porter

Directions

1. Combine the ice cream and Vanilla Porter in a blender.
2. Blend until smooth.
3. Pour into a glass and enjoy.

This drink is great for those hot July and August afternoon games.

—Joshua Lepley and Breckenridge Brewery
Barleydine.com
Williamsport, PA

Playing-in-October Onion Soup

Ingredients

- 3 tablespoons butter
- 1 tablespoon olive oil
- 3 pounds Spanish onions, peeled and thinly sliced
- Salt, to taste
- 1 tablespoon flour
- Dried oregano
- Garlic powder
- 8 cups beef stock (or 4 cups beef and 4 cups chicken)
- 2 cups dry white wine
- Freshly ground black pepper, to taste
- 1 loaf crusty Italian bread
- 8 to 16 ounces good melting cheese, shredded (try a mix of fontina, aged mozzarella, baby Swiss, and/or Gruyère), some reserved for garnish

Directions

At Home

1. Melt butter and oil in a large, heavy pan on medium-low heat.
2. Add onions, cover, and cook, stirring often until onions are very soft, with a little color, but not burnt. Add salt to taste.
3. Reduce heat to medium; add flour, oregano, and garlic powder to taste. Stir (on heat) for 2 to 3 minutes.
4. Stir in 2 cups of stock; add remaining stock and the wine. Season with salt and pepper.
5. Simmer for 30 minutes.

6. Remove from heat, cool, and store in an airtight container for easy transport.
7. Preheat oven to 400°F. Cut the bread into thick slices. (Be sure to cut the bread into slices that will fit into your serving cups/bowls.)
8. Place the slices on a baking sheet and toast for 5 minutes.
9. Remove from the oven and top each slice with shredded cheese.
10. Return to oven and toast until the cheese is completely melted. Remove from the oven and let cool on a rack.
11. Store the croutons in a sealed plastic bag.

In the Parking Lot

12. Simmer soup on the grill or outdoor stove until hot.
13. Place a crouton in an insulated bowl or cup; pour warm soup over.
14. Serve with some extra cheese and bread.

—Maddy Martin
Philadelphia, PA

Acknowledgments

There are many people who contributed to the publishing of this book.

First and foremost, credit is due to the hundreds of thousands of people who make up Phillies Nation. We are a diverse group of fans centered in the Delaware Valley, represented around the world, and united by a common theme: our love for the Philadelphia Phillies.

From this group of diehard fans came all the recipes in this book. We'd like to thank the many chefs who dedicated plenty of pregame time, effort, and money to perfecting these dishes—particularly the restaurant chefs who shared their recipes. Thousands more from Phillies Nation contributed ideas, comments, suggestions, and even potential titles. A few that just missed the cut include Grilladelphia; Burgers, Bumpers, Hot Dogs, and Hangovers; Concrete Kitchen; A South Philly Tradition; and Flavor Nation.

Essays in the opening section were penned by PhilliesNation.com editor-in-chief Pat Gallen and former Citizens Bank Park "Beerman" Nick Staskin. We'd like to extend a big tip of the cap to all PhilliesNation.com writers over the years, including Tim, Rob, Amanda, Corey, Jay, Don, Ian, Kieran, Ryan, Eric, Alex, Paul, Michael, Jon, Ben, Jason, Jonathan, and Jim.

High fives and handshakes go out to friends of Phillies Nation who have contributed to the book and website: Joshua Lepley from Barleydine.com; Garry Maddox; Kelli Amato; Doug Pecht; Jason Lyons; and the crews at IWS and Mindshare.

Of course, I'd like to offer plenty of hugs for my family, including Mom, Dad, Julie, Siti, and Aunt Joan, for their recipes and advice as well as their loving contributions to my cooking and Phillies memories over the years.

And finally, thanks to you for taking the time
to read this book and root for the Phillies.
Go Phils!

—Brian Michael

Brian after the Phillies won the 2008 World Series

About Phillies Nation

Brian Michael founded Phillies Nation as a Phillies blog in 2004—July 25, 2004, to be precise, the day Eric Milton nearly threw a no-hitter. Since then, Phillies Nation has grown into something more than a blog. It is a community for the most fanatical Phillies fans to share ideas, absorb information, and have fun supporting the Phillies.

We host road trips and game-watching parties around the country, and tailgate parties in Philly. We create and sell fun T-shirts with local artists and businesses in Philly. We send care packages to Phillies fans in the military and get involved in other charitable efforts through the Phillies Nation Foundation. We produce a television show uniquely from a fan's perspective. We do all this because we love the Phillies and sharing with fellow fans.

Our writers are analytical and emotional, in the press box and in the stands, all to cover everything Phillies fans need to know about the team they love. Stay updated with the latest news and events by visiting us online:

www.philliesnation.com

www.facebook.com/philliesnation

www.twitter.com/philliesnation

www.youtube.com/philliesnation

About Philabundance

A portion of the proceeds from the sale of this book are being contributed to:

Philabundance reduces hunger and food insecurity in the Delaware Valley by providing food access to people in need, in partnership with organizations and individuals.

Founded in 1984, it is the region's largest hunger-relief organization, providing food to approximately sixty-five thousand people per week—23 percent of them kids and 16 percent seniors.

For more information on how you can help, visit www. philabundance.org or call 215-339-0900.

Driving hunger from our communities

Think you can do better?

Submit your own recipe for the next edition of this cookbook by visiting:

www.philliesnation.com/cookbook

Index

Crawfish Crab Cakes, 76–77